DEGAS BY

Degas

Rosmarie
  zu deinem 22ten
Geburtstag mit
Liebe von Mama
und Papa.
          6.4.91.

KNOPF
75
YEARS·OF·PUBLISHING

Woman Combing her Hair Before the Mirror, c.1877, Norton Simon Art
Foundation, Pasadena

DEGAS
BY

ARTISTS BY THEMSELVES
EDITED BY RACHEL BARNES

ALFRED A. KNOPF
NEW YORK
1990

Originally published in Great Britain by
Webb & Bower (Publishers) Limited, Exeter, Devon

Series devised by Nicky Bird

Designed by Vic Giolitto

Library of Congress Cataloging-in-Publication Data
Barnes, Rachel.
    Artists by themselves. Degas/Rachel Barnes. — 1st American ed.
      p. cm.
    "Originally published in Great Britain by Webb & Bower
(Publishers) Limited, Exeter"—T.p. verso.
    ISBN 0–394–58907–6 : $16.95
    1. Degas, Edgar. 1834–1917—Sources. 2. Painting—Themes.
motives. I. Title.
ND553.D3B37 1990
759.4—dc20   90–52730
                                                 CIP

Manufactured in Italy
First American Edition

CONTENTS

Introduction 6

Degas by Degas 18

Self Portrait 19

Drawing from Donatello's Davide 21

The Daughter of Jephthah 23

View of Naples 25

Horse and Rider 27

Woman with a Vase 29

The Dance Class 31

The Cotton Market, New Orleans 33

Race Horses 35

The Absinthe Drinkers 37

The Ballet Scene from Robert le Diable 39

Beach Scene (Detail) 41

Woman Leaving her Bath 43

Singer with a Glove 45

The Violinist 47

Study for Miss Lala at the Cirque Fernando 49

Lala at the Cirque Fernando 51

Café Concert Singer 53

Four Studies of Dancers 55

The Dance Lesson 57

The Ironer 59

Nude Woman Drying her Hair 61

Nude Woman Drying her Feet 63

Woman Drying Herself 65

Race Horse and Jockey 67

Combing the Hair 69

Sculpture of Dancer of Fourteen Years Old Dressed in Tutu 71

After the Bath 73

Woman Drying her Hair 75

Self Portrait 77

Chronology 78

Acknowledgements 80

INTRODUCTION

My art, what do you want to say about it? Do you think you
can explain the merits of a picture to those who do not see
them? *Dites?* ... I can find the best and clearest words to
explain my meaning, and I have spoken to the most intelligent
people about art, and they have not understood – to B. for
instance; but among people who understand, words are not
necessary, you say humph, he ha, and everything has been
said. My opinion has always been the same. I think that
literature has only done harm to art. You puff out the artist
with vanity you inculcate the taste for notoriety, and that is all;
you do not advance public taste by one jot ... despite all your
scribbling it never was in a worse state than it is at present
... *Dites?*

Edgar Degas' remarks to the Irish journalist and writer George
Moore show his deep aversion to theorizing and intellectualizing
about art. Paintings, he makes it quite clear, are for looking at not
talking about, and he, as an artist, would have chosen words and not
paint had that been his natural medium.

Yet paradoxically – and Degas was frequently self-contradictory
– he was an articulate and often creative writer, and his comments
about his own work and about art in general are highly
illuminating. Considering he was a shy and introspective man, his
letters are also revealing and often unexpectedly emotional, showing
a vulnerable side that only his family and more intimate friends
were allowed to see. His notebooks and diaries are full of thoughts

Dancer Adjusting her Costume, Fitzwilliam Museum, Cambridge

and ideas which throw light upon his working methodology, while his sketchbook notes record his attendances at ballet rehearsals and performances precisely, reinforcing the image of a painter whose art relied on his careful observations of the urban world. Indeed, some of these entries read exactly like verbal transcriptions of a Degas painting:

> A severely truncated dancer, do some arms or legs, or some backs ... corsets that have just been removed ... which retain the form of the body ... the hollowing of the cheeks of the

Young Spartan Girl, c.1860, Musée du Louvre, Paris

> bassoonists . . . different blacks, black veils of deep mourning
> floating on the face – black gloves, mourning carriages . . .
> still lives of different breads, large, oval, long, round, etc.

Degas was also a poet of some ability, influenced by the avant-garde
writers of his time. He once said to the Symbolist poet Stephane
Mallarmé that he found 'the sacred tool' of poetry difficult, and that
he had on occasions spent a whole day working on a sonnet without
making any progress. 'And it isn't ideas which I lack. I have all too
many', he told the poet, to which Mallarmé made the famous reply:

'One does not make sonnets with ideas, Degas, but with words'.

Degas' undoubted feeling for words expressed itself verbally as well as in writing, and he was well known among his circle as something of a wit. He was on friendly terms with Oscar Wilde and James McNeil Whistler, whose conversation in Degas' presence was, according to Wilde, reduced to 'brilliant flashes of silence.'

Degas' writings also reveal his complex and often bewildering personality. In reading his early letters and diary entries one becomes aware of the gradual change from the shy young man, with a tendency to romanticize and fall easily in love, to the final image of the lonely, cynical, almost blind old man, walking alone around Paris at the outbreak of the First World War.

In fact, Degas decided that he did not want to share his life with anyone. There is some indication in his correspondence that as a young man he was badly hurt in love, but later on his all-consuming preoccupation with art left little room for a close relationship. He once said as a joke that he couldn't bear to marry for fear of having his wife say to him, 'That's a nice little thing that you've done this morning' – but the jest clearly contained some germ of truth. Certainly his self-imposed solitude did not always, and perhaps not often, bring him much happiness or peace of mind. In 1896, as an old man, he reflected sadly to his friend Henri Rouart:

Your form of posterity's beginning again. You will be blessed, good man, in your children and the children of your children. Since I have a cold I have been making some reflections on bachelorhood and three-quarters of what I tell myself is sad. I embrace you.

It is also clear that with the onset of old age, and the increasing loneliness and melancholia that accompanied it, Degas regretted his notoriously rude and curt behaviour. In 1890, he wrote to his old colleague Evariste de Valernes:

> I was, or I seemed to be, hard with everyone ... the sort of passion for brutality, which came from uncertainty and my bad humour. I felt more badly made, so badly equipped, so weak, which seemed to me that my calculations on art were right. I brooded against the whole world and myself. I ask your pardon sincerely if, on a pretext of this damned art, I have wounded a very intelligent and fine mind, perhaps even a heart.

Although Degas was associated with the Impressionist group – he exhibited in all but one of the eight shows they held in Paris between 1874 and 1886 – in a number of ways his aims and achievements as an artist were quite disparate. While Monet, Renoir, Pissarro, Sisley and other members of the group were principally concerned with observing the transient effects of light and atmosphere on landscape and water, Degas was far more attracted to the urban life of Paris – his birthplace – and the world of theatres, cafés, the opera, ballet and the racetrack. He was more interested in recording the human figure in motion than in observing natural phenomena. Unlike the Impressionists, he had no interest in painting *en plein air*, preferring either to work before the model in his studio or to visit the Parisian spectacles which so excited his artist's eye.

Degas' major inspirations were the advent of photography, invented by Louis Daguerre in Paris in 1839, and the Japanese print, which had inspired a number of experimental painters since

Horse and Jockey, c. 1887–90, Bibliothèque Nationale, Paris

its discovery by Degas' friend, Georges Braquemonde, in the 1850s. From photography Degas learned to perceive his subject and plan his compositions in an informal way, influenced by early photographic experiments which showed unexpected angles and objects or limbs accidentally severed by the camera. From the 1860s the boldness and directness of the Japanese print also developed his interest in compositions showing an unexpected viewpoint, exemplified in such paintings as 'L'Absinthe' (see p 37). Together with artists and writers like Baudelaire, the Goncourts and Whistler, Degas visited Madame Desoye's shop La Jonque Chinoise in the Rue de Rivoli, which sold Japanese prints and objets d'art.

In his early notebooks Degas constantly stressed the influence and importance of Italy and classical painting, thus emphasizing the distinction between his art and that of the Impressionists who, at least initially, preferred to reject the great masters as formative influences. Degas had made regular trips to Italy from his childhood, as his grandfather lived in Naples and he had an aunt in Florence, and as a young artist he saw the value of making copies of the Renaissance masterpieces, which undoubtedly helped develop his genius as a draughtsman. His taste in Renaissance painting included the Quattrocento, notably Giotto, Perugino and Fra Angelico, but he also loved and studied Titian, Michelangelo and Leonardo, the artists of the High Renaissance. At times in his career he experienced divided loyalties – his adulation of old masters vied with his equally strong fascination with contemporary subjects. 'O, Giotto, don't prevent me from seeing Paris, and you Paris, don't prevent me from seeing Giotto,' he wrote.

Degas was further distinguished from the other Impressionists by his upper middle class background. His inherited family money

The Ballet Class, c. 1880, Philadelphia Museum of Art: W. P. Wilstach Collection

made it much easier for him to experiment at his leisure without the appalling pressure to provide for a family out of his earnings which caused both Monet and Renoir so much discomfort and suffering in the early days. By his own admission, Degas had a snobbish attitude to those he considered inferior, either socially or intellectually, an elitism quite alien to the other painters in the group.

Shortly before the first Impressionist exhibition in 1874, which Degas helped to organize, he started work on one of his most famous themes, the ballet dancers. Despite his fear in later years that he would be remembered merely as 'the painter of ballet dancers', many of these works show Degas at his best, observing movement and light with great acuteness. The earliest paintings of dancers concentrate mainly on performances, classes and rehearsals. By 1878 he was tending to paint and sketch the dancers as individuals; then finally, from the mid-eighties and with the onset of blindness, he worked both on the large pastels and small sculptures.

The last theme Degas explored was his completely original study of the nude in 'Femmes à Leurs Toilette', criticized at the time by Huysman for bringing 'an attentive cruelty and a patient hatred' to the nude. Degas set out to observe women unposed, unselfconscious and unaware of scrutiny, washing, brushing their hair or in the bath tub. Despite Huysman's criticism, Degas does not denigrate or humiliate his models in these domestic studies. Although they are apparently spontaneous, Degas never fails to bring out a natural grace and realism which is far more telling than many of the conventionally posed nudes of the past.

Degas' last years were lonely and isolated, although much of this was self-imposed after the deaths of some of his closest friends, like Rouart, caused him to become even more introspective. The onset of blindness, a tragedy for anyone but for a painter unbearable, made him at times very bitter. Yet, despite his solitude, the scope of his collecting showed that Degas remained appreciative of contemporary developments right up to the end, buying paintings by Toulouse-Lautrec, Gauguin and Van Gogh. All these painters

Madame Hortense Valpinçon (Detail), 1871, Minneapolis Institute of Arts

Portrait Sketches, Bibliothèque Nationale, Paris

were, in their turn, great admirers of Degas' genius. All three suffered a great deal for their art, dying in deep despair, and it is traditional to see the Post-Impressionists as a new generation of painters who suffered, almost inevitably, in order to create. Yet this extract from a letter, written to a friend on the onset of blindness, reveals that Degas also experienced deep unhappiness and isolation for the sake of his art:

If you were single, fifty years of age (for the last month·) you would know similar moments when a door shuts inside one and not only on one's friends. One suppresses everything around one and once all alone one finally kills oneself, out of disgust. I have made too many plans, here I am blocked, impotent . . .

Self Portrait
1855

Musée d'Orsay, Paris

It seems to me that if one wants to be a serious artist today and create an original little niche for oneself, or at least ensure that one preserves the highest degree of innocence of character, one must constantly immerse oneself in solitude. There is too much tittle-tattle. It is as if paintings were made, like speculations on the stock markets, out of the friction among people eager for gain. One has, so to speak, as much need of the mind and ideas of one's neighbour to make anything whatsoever as these businessmen have of the capital of others if they are to make a penny. All this trading sharpens your mind and falsifies your judgment.

... The heart is an instrument which goes rusty if it isn't used. Is it possible to be a heartless artist?

Extract from Degas' notebook

Drawing from Donatello's Davide
1856

Fitzwilliam Museum, Cambridge

... I assure you no art was ever less spontaneous than mine. What I do is the result of reflection and study of the great masters; of inspiration, spontaneity, temperament – temperament is the word – I know nothing.

Reported conversation with Degas

Pb. 2136

94

The Daughter of Jephthah
1859-60

Smith College Museum of Art, Northampton, Mass

... I saw an oriental horse exactly the colour of pink marble slightly dappled reddish-brown violet. – It was rounded like a bronze.

A grey-blue sky of such a tone that the lights can be picked out in light colours and the shadows simply in black. For the red of Jephthah's gown, I must remember the orange-red tones of the old man in Delacroix's picture. The hillside with its dull and blue-green tones. Reduce much of the landscape to patches ... A few heads raised in profile and vivid behind Jephthah.

Greyish pea-green with dirty white striped belt – and a pinkish slate blue veil. – Show the conquered man embracing his daughter.

I don't know if I would change my fate for his for all the gold in the world. In the trophies against the dark sky a lot of harmonies – gold shields with light blue drapery – silver ones – dark blue breast-plates displayed in a bluish olive green ...

Look for Mantegna's spirit and love and Veronese's colouring. The belt on the young man bending down, prepare it in a yellowish grey, then glaze it in green earth. Streak it with dark bluish green.

The man carrying a vase, short dark greyish-blue tunic.

Graduated blue sky – a few white fleecy clouds. The ground at the front in a grey-violet shadow. Middle ground in the light, hills interlocking, chalky and covered in reddish-brown grass, quite high.

Extract from Degas' notebook

[22]

View of Naples

1860

Bibliothèque Nationale, Paris

From memory: at about 5 o'clock in the evening, Castel Sant' Elmo and the town on a slope . . . the Castel dell'Ovo stood out against the pinkish slopes of Vesuvius, which was green and black as in winter. Mosaics in the Museum; how can one forget that the Antique, which is the strongest art, is also the most charming? Colourists like Veronese, audacious and always harmonious.

The shadows are full of play. What resourcefulness in their relation to each other.

Thus a deep blue sky behind a face is worked up to infinity by tones of turquoise, lilac, pink – what variety.

This mosaic near the window representing a man sitting on a ram crossing the water, with a woman raising an exquisite arm, is a delightful and skilful sketch.

Truly I can think of nothing which gives a better idea of this harmony than a beautiful and vivid Veronese, grey as silver and coloured like blood. If I had my box of pastels I would learn a lesson from it which would last me a lifetime. It is Phryxos – and Hellé his sister.

I recall that as I was passing through Crau I came across everything I imagined a desert to be, the warm grey ground dotted with stones covering a little grass.

Tiny ponds green as an unripe lemon. The slightly troubled sea was greenish-grey, the foam on the waves silver – the sea was disappearing into a haze. The sky was grey, the Castello dell'Ovo stood out in a mass of golden green. The boats on the sand were specks of dark sepia.

Extract from Degas' notebook

Horse and Rider
1867

Musée du Louvre, Paris

It is the movement of people and things that distracts and even consoles, if there is still consolation to be had for one so unhappy. If the leaves of the trees did not move, how sad the trees would be and we too!

Letter to Henri Rouart, 1855

Woman with a Vase
1872

Musée d'Orsay, Paris

Make portraits of people in typical, familiar poses, being sure above all to give their faces the same kind of expression as their bodies. Thus if laughter typifies an individual, make her laugh. – There are, of course, feelings which one cannot convey, out of propriety, as portraits are not intended for us painters alone. How many delicate nuances to put in.

Extract from Degas' notebook

The Dance Class
1873

Musée d'Orsay, Paris

She dances, dying. As around the reed
Of a flute where the sad wind of Weber plays,
The ribbon of her steps twists and knots,
Her body sinks and falls in the movement of a bird.

The violins sing. Fresh from the blue of the water
Silvana comes, and carefully ruffles and preens:
The happiness of rebirth and love on her cheeks,
In her eyes, on her breasts, on her whole new being . . .

And her satin feet like needles embroider
Patterns of pleasure. The springing girl
Wears out my poor eyes, straining to follow her.

With a trifle, as always, the beautiful mystery ends.
She bends back her legs too far in a leap,
It's the leap of a frog in the Cytherean pond.

Sonnet by Degas

The Cotton Market, New Orleans
1873

Musée d'Orsay, Paris

I have attached myself to a fairly vigorous picture, which is destined for Agnew (the English picture dealer) and which he should place in Manchester. For if a spinner ever wished to find his painter, he really ought to hit upon me. The Interior of a Cotton Buyers' Office in New Orleans.

In it are about fifteen individuals more or less occupied with a table covered with the precious material, and two men, one half-leaning and the other half-sitting on it; the buyer and the broker are discussing a pattern. A raw picture if there ever was one . . .

Letter to James Tissot, 1873

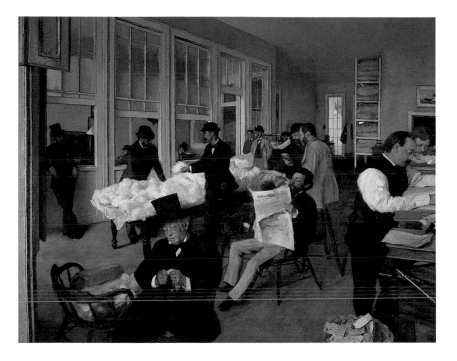

Race Horses
1873–5

Museum of Fine Arts, Boston

Now, while at the time I was reasonably well acquainted with 'the noblest conquest ever made by man', while I happened fairly frequently to mount one and had no great difficulty in telling the difference between a pure-bred and a half-bred, whereas I was quite familiar with the anatomy and myology of the animal, which I had studied on one of those anatomical models to be found in any plaster-caster's premises, I was totally ignorant of the mechanism that regulated a horse's movements. I knew infinitely less on the subject than a non-commissioned officer whose lengthy and attentive practice enables him to visualize the animal's reactions and reflexes, even when he is speaking of an absent horse.

Marey had not yet invented the device which made it possible to decompose the movements – imperceptible to the human eye – of a bird in flight, of a galloping or trotting horse. For his studies of horses, which are so sincere and which he used in his military canvases, Meissonier was reduced to parking his carriage for hours on end on the Champs-Elysées. There, alongside the footpath, he would study the horsemen and their handsome, frisky horses. Thus, this bad painter was one of the best informed on horses that I have ever met.

Cited in Thiebault-Sisson
Degas Sculpteur, 1921

The Absinthe Drinkers
1875–6

Musée d'Orsay, Paris

A painting is above all a product of the artist's imagination, it must never be a copy. If, at a later stage, he wants to add two or three touches from nature, of course it doesn't spoil anything. But the air one sees in the paintings of the masters is not the air one breathes.

Reported conversation with Degas

The Ballet Scene from Robert le Diable
1876

Victoria and Albert Museum, London

Shadow carried from the score on to the rounded back of the rostrum – dark grey background – bowstring brightly lit by the lamps, head of Georges in silhouette, light red shadows – flesh tones.

In the receding arches the moonlight barely licks the columns – on the ground the effect pinker and warmer than I made it – black vault, the beams indistinct . . .

The tops of the footlights are reflected by the lamps – trees much greyer, mist around the receding arcades – the last nuns more in flannel colour but more indistinct – in the foreground, the arcades are greyer and merge into one another . . .

The receding vault is black, apart from a little reflection in the centre . . .

The theatre boxes a mass of dark lacquered brick red – in the director's box, light red pink face, striking shirts, vivid black.

Near the lamp a dancer from behind on her knees, light falls only on her skirt. The back and the rest in quite deep shadow – striking effect.

Extract from Degas' notebook

Beach Scene (Detail)
1876-7

National Gallery, London

It is all very well to copy what you see, but it is much better to draw only what you still see in your memory. This is a transformation in which imagination collaborates with memory. Then you only reproduce what has struck you, that is to say the essential, and so your memories and your fantasy are freed from the tyranny which nature holds over them. That is why pictures made in this way by a man who has cultivated his memory, knowing both the old masters and his craft well, are practically always remarkable. Look at Delacroix.

Cited in Georges Jeanniot
'Souvenirs sur Degas' in *Revue Universelle*

Woman Leaving her Bath
1877

Pastel, Musée d'Orsay, Paris

See how different the times are for us; two centuries ago, I would have painted 'Susannah Bathing', now I just paint 'Woman in a Tub'.

Reported conversation with Degas

Singer with a Glove
1878

To work a great deal at evening effects, lamps, candles, etc. The fascinating thing is not to show the source of light, but the effect of light. That side of art today could become immense – is it possible not to see?

Extract from Degas' notebook

The Violinist
1878-9

Museum of Fine Arts, Boston

Series on instruments and instrumentalists, their forms, the twisting of the hands and arms and neck of a violinist; for example, swelling out and hollowing of the cheeks of the bassoonists, oboeists, etc.

Do a series in aquatint on *mourning*, different blacks – black veils of deep mourning floating on the face – black gloves – mourning carriages, Undertakers' vehicles – carriages like Venetian gondolas.

On smoke – smokers' smoke, pipes, cigarettes, cigars – smoke from locomotives, from tall factory chimneys, from steam boats etc. Smoke compressed under bridges – steam.

On evening – infinite variety of subjects in cafés – different tones of the glass globes reflected in the mirrors.

On bakery, *Bread* – Series on bakers' boys, seen in the cellar itself, or through the basement windows from the street – backs the colour of pink flour – beautiful curves of dough – still lifes of different breads, large, oval, long, round, etc. Studies in colour of the yellows, pinks, greys, whites of bread.

Extract from Degas' notebook

Study for Miss Lala at the Cirque Fernando
1879

Tate Gallery, London

Art is the same world as artifice, that is to say, something deceitful.
It must succeed in giving the impression of nature by false means,
but it has to look true. Draw a straight line askew, as long as it gives
the impression of being straight!

Reported conversation with Degas

[49]

Lala at the Cirque Fernando
1879

National Gallery, London

I have always tried to urge my colleagues to seek for new combinations along the path of draughtsmanship, which I consider a more fruitful field than that of colour. But they wouldn't listen to me and have gone the other way.

Reported conversation with Walter Sickert, 1885

Café Concert Singer
1879

Norton Simon Art Foundation, Pasadena

My dear Lerolle, go at once to hear Thérésa at the Alcazar, rue du Faubourg-Poissonnière.

It is near the conservatoire and it is better. It has already been said, a long time ago – I do not know what man of taste said it – that she should be put on to Gluck. At the moment you are all absorbed in Gluck. It is the right moment to go and hear this admirable artist.

She opens her large mouth and there emerges the most roughly, the most delicately, the most spiritually tender voice imaginable. And the soul, and the good taste, where could one find better? It is admirable.

Letter to Henri Lerolle, 1883

Four Studies of Dancers
1879

Musée du Louvre, Paris

But it's true, isn't it, Pauline, that people imagine that artists and their models spend their time getting up to all sorts of obscenities? As far as work goes, well, they paint or sculpt when they're tired of enjoying themselves . . . And when people talk of ballet dancers they imagine them as being covered with jewellery and lavishly maintained with a mansion, carriage and servants, just as it says in story books. In reality most of them are poor girls doing a very demanding job and who find it very difficult to make ends meet . . . I've got to know these little ballet pupils since they've been coming to pose for me.

Cited in Alice Michel
Degas and his Model

The Dance Lesson
1879

The Metropolitan Museum of Art, New York

We go on stage, he walks across the hall, followed by his staff: he takes a place in the middle with the jury. The whole hall in darkness, large green-grey cloths covering the boxes and the stalls. Six big gas lights on stands with large reflectors in the orchestra pit. It begins. The little boys in their little black or blue jackets, short trousers, white socks. Looking like urchins. Fr Mérante standing on the left playing the violin. First group of little girls. Mme Théodore on the right with a violin playing quite out of tune. Second group, I recognize Guerra with Mme Théodore. Third, Mme Théodore standing on the right. It is the age when dancing is pretty, it is naive, primitive, firm. The jury claps frequently. Fourth group. In a *pas de trois*, a dancer falls and remains on the ground, cries, she is surrounded, carried away by her arms and legs, sadness. Mérante, then Vaucorbeil, then Meyer, then, etc climb on the stage by a little staircase by the corner of the orchestra pit. It seems like just a sprain. Mérante announces it. Everyone recovers. The exam is very successful, people clap often. Curious silhouettes around me, in front of me. Fifth group, Mme Mérante on the left, behind her a violinist and a viola player sitting, music stand behind which, since the beginning, Pluque has been sheltering from the footlights. A bow, it is over. People come back on the stage, everybody, parents, teachers, jury, etc ... excited dancers. The classes are set up. Thanks addressed to Vaucorbeil. We return. Mérante on familiar terms.

Notes on a dance examination from Degas' notebook

[56]

The Ironer

1884

Musée d'Orsay, Paris

After having done portraits seen from above, I will do some from below – sitting very close to a woman and looking at her from below I shall see her head glossy and surrounded with crystals. Do simple things, such as drawing a profile which does not move, moving oneself up or down, and the same for a whole body – a piece of furniture, a whole room. Do a series of arm movements in a dance or legs which do not move, turning oneself . . . Finally study a figure or an object, it does not matter which, from every viewpoint. One could use a mirror for that without changing one's position. Only the glass would be lowered or made to lean forward. One would turn round. Ideas for the studio. To put steps all round the room to get accustomed to drawing things from above and from below. Only paint things seen in the glass to get used to a hatred of *trompe l'oeil* effects.

Extract from Degas' notebook

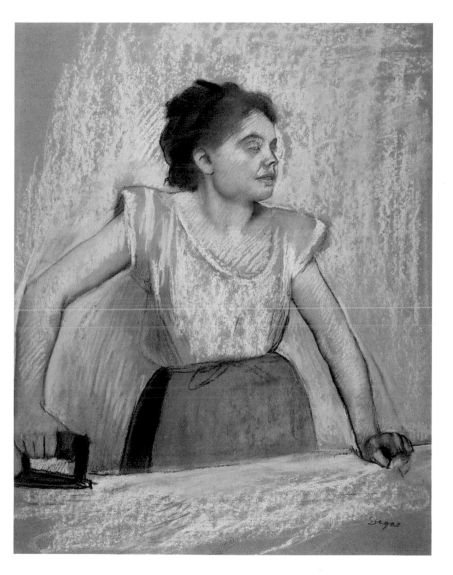

Nude Woman Drying her Hair
1885

Musée d'Orsay, Paris

What use is my mind? granted that it enables me to hail a bus and pay my fare. But once I am inside my studio, what use is my mind? I have my model, my pencil, my paper, my paints. My mind doesn't interest me.

Reported conversation with Degas

Nude Woman Drying her Feet
1885

Musée du Louvre, Paris

Hitherto the nude has always been represented in poses which presuppose an audience, but these women of mine are honest, simple folk, unconcerned by any other interests than those involved in their physical condition. Here is another; she is washing her feet. It is as if you looked through the keyhole.

Reported conversation with Degas

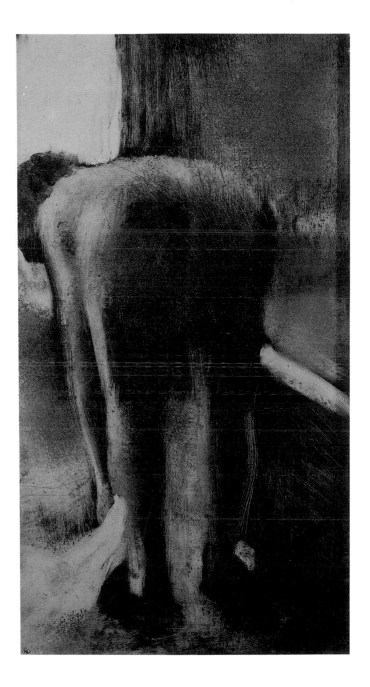

Woman Drying Herself

Late 1880s-Early 1890s

National Gallery, London

A picture demands a certain mystery, vagueness, fantasy. If one dots all the i's one ends by being boring. Even in front of nature, one must compose. There are people who believe that this is forbidden. Corot must have composed in front of nature, too. His charm derives above all from that. A picture is an original combination of lines and tones which make themselves felt.

Extract from Degas' notebook

Race Horse and Jockey
c. 1887-90

Museum Boymans-van Beuningen, Rotterdam

The older I became, the more clearly I realized that to achieve exactitude so perfect in the representation of animals that a feeling of life is conveyed, one had to go into three dimensions, not merely because the activity itself requires prolonged observation from the artist and more sustained attention, but also because this is an area in which approximations are unacceptable. The most beautiful and the best-wrought drawing is always less than the precise, the absolute truth and thus leaves the way open to all that is fraudulent. You know the much-vaunted and, in fact, very worthy drawing in which Fromentin captures the stride of a galloping Arabian steed; compare it with reality and you will be struck far less by what it expresses than by all that it lacks. The natural disposition and true character of the animal are absent from this enthusiastic improvisation by a very clever hand.

Cited in Thiebault-Sisson
Degas Sculpteur, 1921

Combing the Hair
1892–5

National Gallery, London

Thus it is not instinct alone which makes us say that it is in colouring that one must look everywhere for the affinity between what is living and what is dead or vegetal. I can easily bring to mind certain hair colouring, for example, because it struck me as being the colour of varnished walnut or tow, or like horse-chestnut bark, real hair with its suppleness and lightness or its hardness and heaviness. And then one paints in so many different ways, on so many different surfaces that the same tone will appear as one thing here and another there. I am not speaking of contrasts which would distort it in an entirely different way.

Extract from Degas' notebook

Sculpture of Dancer of Fourteen Years Old Dressed in Tutu
Undated

Musée d'Orsay, Paris

... The only reason that I made wax figures of animals and humans was for my own satisfaction, not to take time off from painting or drawing, but in order to give my paintings and drawings greater expression, greater ardour and more life. They are exercises to get me going; documentary, preparatory motions, nothing more. None of this is intended for sale. Can you see me designing my studies of horses after the fashion of a Frémiet, with such wealth of picturesque detail, which never fails to startle the middle classes? Or can you see me bending my studies of nudes into attitudes of false elegance, like Carrier-Belleuse? You will never catch me scratching the back of a torso nor revelling in the palpitating flesh that you critics are always caressing when you speak of the academic sculptors of the Institut. What matters to me is to express nature in all of its aspects, movement in its exact truth, to accentuate bone and muscle and the compact firmness of flesh. My work is no more than irreproachable in its construction. As for the *frisson* of flesh – what a trifle! My sculptures will never convey that feeling of completeness that is the *ne plus ultra* for the makers of statues, because after all, nobody will see these experiments, nobody will take it into their heads to talk about them, not even yourself. Before I die, all of this will disintegrate of its own accord and it will be just as well, as far as my reputation is concerned ...

Cited in Thiebault-Sisson
Degas Sculpteur, 1921

[71]

After the Bath
1895

Philadelphia Museum of Art
Purchased: Estate of the late George D. Widener

'Oh! Women can never forgive me; they hate me, they can feel that I am disarming them. I show them without their coquetry, in the state of animals cleaning themselves!'

'You think they don't like you?'

'I am sure of it; they see in me the enemy. Fortunately, for if they did like me, that would be the end of me!'

Cited in Georges Jeanniot
The Memories of Degas, 1933

Woman Drying her Hair
1905–7

Norton Simon Art Foundation, Pasadena

My sight especially (health is the most valuable of all our possessions) is not right. You remember one day that you said in speaking of I don't know whom, that in growing old he no longer 'made connections', a term used in medicine for feeble brains. This term is one I have always remembered. My sight no longer 'makes connections' or with such difficulty that I am often tempted to give everything up and sleep forever. It is also true that the weather is so variable; when it is dry and clear I see better, very sensibly, although it takes me some time to get used to the strong light, which wounds me in spite of my smoked glasses; but as soon as the humidity returns I am like today; my eyes, which were burning yesterday, are swimming today. Will this ever come to an end, and how?

Undated letter to Henri Rouart

Self Portrait
1865

Calouste Gulbenkian Foundation, Lisbon

If you were a bachelor and fifty years old (for a month) you would have moments like these when you would slam yourself like a door, and not only upon your friends. You would suppress everything around you, and once quite alone, you would annihilate yourself, kill yourself even, with disgust. I have begun too many projects which I, myself, have blocked, powerless. And then I have lost the thread. I thought there would always be time. What I did not do, what I was prevented from doing, I never, even in the middle of my worries and in spite of my sick eyes, despaired of being able to do again some beautiful morning.

I piled all my plans in a cupboard for which I myself always carried the key. And I have lost the key. In short I only feel the comatose state I am in and I cannot arouse myself from it. I shall occupy myself, as people say who do nothing. And that is all.

I write you all this without any great need. It is enough to beg your pardon humbly for my rudeness.

Letter to Henri Lerolle, 1884

CHRONOLOGY

Edgar Degas
1834-1917

1834   Born in Paris, the eldest of five children.

1845   Studies at the Lycée Louis le Grand, where he meets Henri Rouart.

1854   First trip to Naples.

1858   Expedition from Rome to Florence.

1859   Returns to Paris and works in studio in Rue Madame found by his family.

1860   Discovers Japanese art.

1868   Beginning of his interest in theatre and ballet.

1874   Father dies in Naples, leaving financial debt for Degas and his brother.
First exhibition of the Impressionists opens, with Degas involved in its organization.

1876   Second Impressionist exhibition at Durand-Ruel's Gallery.

1880   Visit to Spain. Works with Mary Cassatt.

1882   Beginning of his interest in the 'Laundresses'.

1885   Eyesight starting to deteriorate.

1886 Visits Naples on family business. Exhibits 'Femmes à Leurs Toilette' at the eighth Impressionist exhibition. Gives Durand-Ruel the exclusive rights to his works.

1893 First one-man show at Durand-Ruel.

1895-8 Degas preoccupied with series of 'Women Bathing' and working on large scale pastels.

1904 Eyesight deteriorates to the extent that he can only work on sculptures and large compositions. Becomes increasingly introspective and reclusive.

1912 Death of his best friend Rouart, which affects Degas deeply.

Leaves his house in Rue Victor Masse where he has lived for twenty years, which depresses him further.

1914 Degas paintings are accepted at the Louvre in the Camondo collection.

1917 Dies on 27 September and is buried in the family vault in Montmartre cemetery.

ACKNOWLEDGEMENTS

The editor and publishers would like to thank the following for their help in providing the photographs of paintings reproduced in this book:

Bibliothèque Nationale, Paris (pp11, 16, 25)
Bridgeman Art Library (p33)
Calouste Gulbenkian Foundation, Lisbon (p77)
Fitzwilliam Museum, Cambridge (pp7, 21)
Fogg Art Museum, Harvard University, Cambridge, Mass (p45)
Metropolitan Museum of Art, New York (p57)
Minneapolis Institute of Art (p15)
Museum Boymans-van Beuningen, Rotterdam (p67)
Museum of Fine Arts, Boston (pp35, 47)
National Gallery, London (pp41, 51, 65, 69)
Norton Simon Art Foundation, Pasadena (frontispiece, pp53, 75)
Philadelphia Museum of Art (pp13, 73)
Photo RMN (cover, pp8, 19, 27, 29, 31, 37, 43, 55, 59, 61, 63, 71)
Smith College Museum of Art, Northampton, Mass (p23)
Tate Gallery, London (p49)
Victoria & Albert Museum, London (p39)

We would also like to thank the publishers of the following books for access to the material contained in them which has been reproduced in this volume:

Degas' Letters edited by Mariel Guerin and translated by Marguerite Kay, Bruno Cassiter, Oxford 1947
The Notebooks of Edgar Degas T. Reff, Clarendon Press, Oxford 1976
Degas Sculpteur Thiebault-Sisson 1921
Degas and his Model Alice Michel
The Memories of Degas George Jeanniot 1933

Every effort has been made to contact the owners of the copyright of all the information contained in this book, but if, for any reason, any acknowledgements have been omitted, the publishers ask those concerned to contact them.